003457

Text copyright © 1995 Jeanne Willis
Illustrations copyright © 1995 Roger Wade Walker

The right of Jeanne Willis to be identified as
the author of this Work and the right of
Roger Wade Walker to be identified as the
illustrator of this work has been asserted to them
in accordance with the Copyright, Designs and
Patents Act 1988.

This edition first published in Great Britain in
1995 by Macdonald Young Books

Photoset in 16/24 Meridien

Printed and bound in Belgium by Proost N.V.

Macdonald Young Books
Campus 400
Maylands Avenue
Hemel Hempstead HP2 7EZ

British Library Cataloguing in Publications Data available

ISBN 0 7500 1709 0
ISBN 0 7500 1710 4 (pb)

Jeanne Willis

Wilbur and Orville take off

Illustrated by Roger Wade Walker

MACDONALD YOUNG BOOKS

1
The Chinese flying top
Dayton, Ohio... about 120 years ago

The Reverend Wright turned into
Hawthorn Street and opened his front
door. He was hiding a surprise.

"Hi, boys. I'm home!" he called.
Wilbur and his little brother, Orville, ran
to greet him.

"What's in the bag, Pa? Is it sweets?"

The Reverend Wright handed over
the parcel and smiled.

Wilbur unwrapped it carefully. His eyes lit up. "Wow! Look at this!" He fingered the tiny propeller. "This bit goes round and round! What on earth is it?"

"Let me see," insisted Orville, standing on tiptoe.

"It's a Chinese flying top," explained their father, "you pull this string, which makes these blades whizz round and then up she goes."

Wilbur raised his eyebrows. "What...do you mean like a bird?"

"The man in the shop reckons it flies like a demon," said the Reverend Wright.

"Come on," whooped Wilbur, "let's try it out in the yard!"

The boys raced outside. "Hey, don't yank the string so hard," said Orville, "here, give it to me. I bet it won't work anyway."

Wilbur held it in his cupped hands as if it was a fledgeling afraid to try its wings.

"Let it go!" yelled Orville. Wilbur pulled the cord. The propeller buzzed into life and the wind sucked the brightly-coloured flying top up into the clouds.

"It's magic," gasped Orville, clapping his hands. "Quick," shouted Wilbur, "after it! It's going to crash into the apple tree."

Too late. Orville found Wilbur crouched over it in the long grass.

"Is it dead, Wil?" he asked, sadly. Wilbur examined it slowly.

"I can probably fix it," he said, "in fact, I'm going to make an even better one."

Wilbur was good at fixing things. Orville watched, fascinated, as his big brother experimented with wood, glue and string.

"I wish we could fly," Orville sighed.

"Lots of people have wished that," said Wilbur, "but we'd need a huge machine. How could a machine heavier than air ever fly?"

Orville pointed to Wilbur's bigger, better version of the Chinese flying top hovering happily over their roof.

"That's heavier than air," he announced, "and that flies."

The hairs on the back of Wilbur's neck tingled with excitement.

"You're right!" he exclaimed, "you're absolutely right!"

Maybe their wish wasn't as impossible as it seemed.

2
Teamwork

The years flew by. The Chinese top lay gathering dust. For a while, the boys put their fascination with flying back in the top drawer.

Orville was standing in the kitchen operating his latest gadget – a home-made printing press, when Wilbur came in with a pair of ice skates.

"Ma says to tell you that Mr Conway wants another four dozen leaflets printed for his hardware shop," he said.

"You ought to do this for a living."

"I intend to," said Orville, "when does he want them by?"

"Noon tomorrow."

"Noon!" exclaimed Orville, "I'm only halfway through the stuff for Cresswell's Candystore…Give us a hand, Wil."

"Sorry, got an ice-hockey match to get to," said Wilbur.

A few hours later, there was a knock at the door. It was the captain of the hockey team.

"What's wrong...where's Wilbur?" asked his mother. There had been an accident. Wilbur had been hit in the face during the match and lost all his front teeth.

"You O.K?" asked Orville. Wilbur seemed so down, Orville was convinced it wasn't just his teeth that were bothering him.

"Don't tell Ma, will you?" whispered his brother, "she'll worry."

"Tell her what?"

"The doctor said I've got something wrong with my heart."

For over two years, Wilbur was forced to live like an invalid. Then just as he was beginning to get better, Mrs. Wright became seriously ill.

Despite Wilbur's desperate efforts to nurse her, Ma went from bad to worse. He was only twenty-two when she died.

The two boys clung to each other. "I can't bear it, Wil," sobbed Orville.

"I know," said Wilbur, gently, "at least we've got each other...We'll be all right. You know that newspaper you always wanted to run? I could do it with you."

"Could you?" Orville smiled through his tears. "Would you? Are you well enough? Only I'd really like that! We could print it too, couldn't we?"

"Course we could."

As soon as they left school, they went into business together.

The newspaper venture was running very smoothly when suddenly a girl rode past the window on a brand new bicycle.

"Did you see that!" exclaimed Wilbur.

"What, the girl?" laughed Orville.

"Not the girl, the bike! It's fantastic!"

They ran outside to have a closer look.

3
Big enough to carry a man

Wilbur and Orville decided bicycles were even better news than the newspaper business. They promptly shut down their printing press and made and sold bikes instead.

The Wright Cycle Company did a roaring trade.

Early one morning, the paper boy
came in with a puncture. "Hi," said
Orville, "what's the latest, apart from
you riding over a nail?"

"Nothing much," said the lad, "two
robberies. Oh, yeah, and some guy
crashed his glider." Wilbur put down the
tyre he was fixing.

"Lilienthal? Is he O.K?" "No, sir," said
the paperboy, "he's dead."

Orville shook his head sadly. "Did you hear that, Wil?" he sighed. They had been following Lilienthal's progress for some years now. Only recently they had leapt up and down with excitement upon hearing that he'd managed to fly an unbelievable one hundred metres. "Otto was so close!" Wilbur mused, "he was about to put an engine in, too."

"Reckon it would have worked?" asked Orville.

Wilbur shrugged, "If we had more information, I bet we could suss it out. Coming to the library with me?"

The best book available was by a gliding enthusiast called Octave Chanute.

"You know," said Wilbur, "if Otto's glider hadn't tipped from side to side, he'd still be alive."

"Fine, but how can something heavier than air stay balanced?" wondered Orville. The answer came to them as they were walking in the hills.

"Crimony!" yelled Orville.

"Have you hurt yourself?" asked Wilbur.

"No...look at that hawk...look what happens to its wings when it catches the wind. See, it's doing it again!"

Wilbur watched. "That's it! That's our answer." The bird was changing the shape of its wings to steady itself during flight.

"We could get a glider to do that," said Wilbur. "We need cord. Lots of cord!"

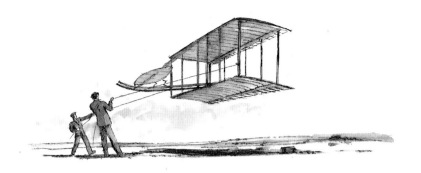

Straight away, they set about building a double-decker kite with cords attached to each corner. They took it out to a field to test it.

"O.K," said Wilbur, "pull! No, down a bit...left a bit...that's it."

Sure enough, when the cords were pulled in the right direction it was possible to control the kite easily.

"It works!" Wilbur punched the air with delight.

"Now what?" grinned Orville.

"We build a glider big enough to carry a man!"

4
Out of this world

By September, the glider was ready. But where were you supposed to fly a thing like that?

"Let's write to Chanute," said Orville, "he'll know."

Shortly after, a letter arrived.

"Chanute says to try Kittyhawk, in North Carolina," said Wilbur. "It's got a weather bureau, life saving stations, oh…and plenty of wind, apparently."

They packed straight away.

"Ah…who's going to look after the shop?" enquired Wilbur, throwing his toothbrush into a bag.

Orville rolled his eyes. "Oh, all right, you go on ahead. I'll sort things out this end."

By the time Orville arrived, Wilbur had set up camp. The glider was sitting on the sand.

"Hello, beauty," said Orville.

Wilbur stuck his head out of the tent. "You talking to me?" he laughed. "Listen, you don't mind if we have an early night, do you? It's going to be a big day tomorrow."

Next morning, Orville was woken by the wind howling outside the tent.

"Coffee, Wil?" he yawned. Wilbur was snoring. Orville peered out of the tent flaps to look at their beloved glider. His jaw dropped.

"Wilbur! Wilbur, wake up. It's vanished!"

The glider was buried under twenty centimetres of sand.

"Start digging," yelled Wilbur, scrabbling with his fingers.

"The front rudder's not damaged," shouted Orville, "how's the upper wing?"

"O.K, I think! I can't believe it's still in one piece."

They dragged the glider across the
dunes, battling against gale-force winds.

"We can't go up in this," groaned
Wilbur, "we'll kill ourselves."

"Let's weigh her down with chains
and see how she goes."

That afternoon, the wind dropped.
It was time for the first manned gliding
session at Killdevil Hills.

"I'll fetch Bill," said Orville.

Bill the Postmaster had agreed to be their flight assistant. He came panting over the sand dunes and shook both young men by the hand. "Scared, fellas?" he asked.

Orville shook his head and beamed.
He crawled onto the lower wing and
gripped with his fingertips. The wind
toyed with the glider, teasing its tail.
"Hold on, little brother," said Wilbur,
breaking into a run. The craft gathered
speed. Suddenly the wind whipped
under its wings and snatched the glider
up, up into the air.

"How does it feel?" yelled Wilbur.

"Out of this world," said a small voice.

"I can't look," whispered Bill, "he's
going to crash!"

5
Let's go for it

Incredibly, neither brother ended up
with so much as a bruise.

"How long were we up, Bill?" asked
Wilbur.

"Two minutes," he replied.

"That's nothing to what we're going
to do next year," said Orville.

Unfortunately, the next year, 1901,
was a disaster. The new plane was no
use and nearly killed Wilbur.

"Come on, let's have another go," insisted Orville. "We might as well risk it."

"Don't be so stupid," snapped Wilbur, "you saw what happened yesterday, the glider stalled. It's a death trap, that thing."

"Pardon me for speaking," sulked Orville, "now where are you going?"

"Home," said Wilbur," all this…it's just a silly schoolboy dream. The calculations are all over the shop."

When Chanute heard Wilbur had given up, he went to see him.

"You must carry on," he insisted, "you know more about flying than anyone. Listen, I want you to give a talk to The Western Society of Civil Engineers. Tell them all you know... please!"

"Come on, Wilbur," insisted Orville, "I'll lend you my best suit."

Eventually, Wilbur agreed. He gave an inspired lecture, questioning all the figures ever published on flight, insisting that he and his brother knew better.

"Brilliant," said Orville, "only you do realise we are going to have to prove the Wrights are right or we'll never live it down."

"No problem," said Wilbur, "we're going to build a windtunnel and test wing shapes, wind speed, everything."

"We are?" Soon, the Wright brothers had the formula for the best flying machine ever.

"Kittyhawk, here we come!" said Orville.

"Hold it. We need an engine," said Wilbur, "no one's got one small enough."

"So we build it," said Orville.

That December, they were standing on Kittyhawk Sands with a brand new flying machine, complete with engine and propeller.

"Who's going to be the pilot?" asked Wilbur, "shall we toss for it?"

"Heads!" said Orville, as the coin spun in the air.

"Darn…Heads it is," grumbled Wilbur, squeezing his brother's hand.

Orville slid into place on the lower wing. Wilbur released the wire. The plane shot forward. It climbed…it stalled. Then it caught a wing and came to a crunching halt.

"You O.K?" called Wilbur.

"Never mind me, what about the plane?" yelled Orville. Luckily Orville wasn't hurt and the plane could easily be fixed.

Three days later, despite dangerous conditions, they were itching to try again.

"Let's go for it!" said Wilbur.

This time, he flew seven hundred and thirty metres. They were triumphant.

The next day, Pa received a telegram;
'SUCCESS. FOUR FLIGHTS. THURSDAY
MORNING. STARTED FROM LEVEL
WITH ENGINE POWER ALONE.
LONGEST FLIGHT 59 SECONDS.
INFORM PRESS. HOME FOR
CHRISTMAS. WILBUR AND ORVILLE.'

6
I can't believe that this is happening

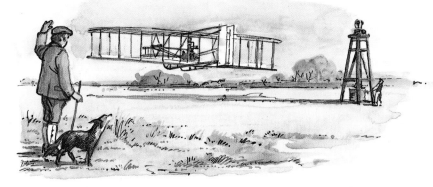

After that, there was no stopping them.
Their planes became more and more
sophisticated and their antics more
daring.

"Yoo hoo, Amos!" hollered Orville as
he swooped low over the field they used
for practice flights.

The old farmer wasn't impressed.
"The boys are at it again," he muttered
to his dog.

By 1905 they had built a plane which flew 39 kilometres in 38 minutes.

"We've achieved the impossible!" admitted Wilbur.

"Look," said Orville, waving an envelope, "I've got an invitation to the United States Trials. They want me to give them a show."

"Snap," said Wilbur, "they want me to do the same in France. I'm leaving in the morning for Le Mans." At last they were getting the recognition they deserved.

Both trials took the crowds by storm. Then came terrible news.

"Monsieur Wright," said an anxious French official, "please sit down. I have something to tell you...your brother...he has crashed at Fort Meyer. His passenger, I'm afraid, was killed."

"And Orville?" asked Wilbur. The official held up his hands and frowned. "Touch and go, Monsieur...so sorry."

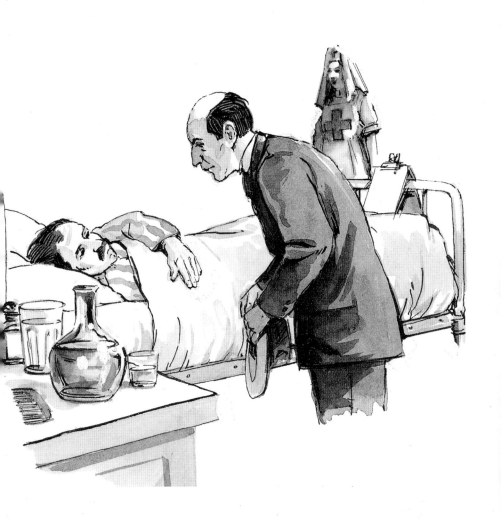

Wilbur cancelled the trials
immediately and rushed to Orville's
bedside. "I'm here, now," he said,
"please get better."

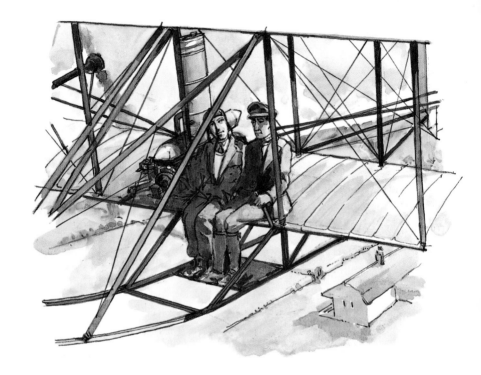

Happily, Orville pulled through. He joined his brother in France and found him very busy training pilots to fly their planes.

"How come you always sleep in the aeroplane hangar," he teased, "the hotels in Paris are terrific."

"I've entertained some very distinguished guests here, I'll have you know," laughed Wilbur. "Like?" said Orville.

"Like Edward the Seventh."

"The King of England? You're kidding!"

It was true. The Wright Brothers were world famous. Their invention was transforming the lives of millions of people. Despite all the royal visits and flashy medals, nothing could beat the party thrown for them by their hometown of Dayton.

The celebrations lasted for two days. As the candle-lit procession wound its way up the little street where they used to play, Orville turned to his brother.

"I can't believe this is happening," he murmured, "if only Ma could see us now."

"Maybe she can," said Wilbur, gazing up at the stars, "maybe she can."